# Spring, 1836: Selected Poems

Other book collections by Arthur Porges:

*Three Porges Parodies and a Pastiche* (1988)
*The Mirror and Other Strange Reflections* (2002)
*Eight Problems in Space: The Ensign De Ruyter Stories* (2008)
*The Adventures of Stately Homes and Sherman Horn* (2008)
*The Calabash of Coral Island and Other Early Stories* (2008)
*The Miracle of the Bread and Other Stories* (2008)

Forthcoming titles by Arthur Porges:

*The Devil and Simon Flagg and Other Fantastic Tales*
*The Ruum and Other Science Fiction Stories*
*The Collected Essays of Arthur Porges*

# Spring, 1836: Selected Poems

## Arthur Porges

### Edited by Richard Simms

Richard Simms Publications

This paperback first edition published in 2008

Richard Simms Publications, Surrey, England

ISBN: 978-0-9556942-2-6

*With special thanks to Sue Wakefield, Cele Porges and Joel Hoffman.*

For more information please visit The Arthur Porges Fan Site:

http://arthurporges.atwebpages.com

# Contents

# Introduction

From the late 1980s onwards, Arthur Porges, a resident of Pacific Grove, contributed a substantial number of writings to his local newspaper, *The Monterey Peninsula Herald* (known today as *The Monterey County Herald*). His work appeared on a frequent basis. In the 1986 to 1989 period, the paper published some forty-odd of his essays in *Weekend*, a supplement magazine to the Sunday edition of the *Herald*. More of Arthur's essays, articles and memoirs followed in the 1990s, with his witty and opinionated correspondence continuing to entertain readers of the letters column in daily issues of the newspaper until a few weeks before he passed away in May 2006.

But his most sustained body of work for the *Herald* was in the form of poetry. The editors loved the quirky, original material he contributed, resulting in a highly productive period for Porges. It is in the pages of this local newspaper that the vast majority of his verse output was published. With this in mind, it is readily apparent that many fans of Arthur's short stories will be largely unaware of his work in this particular field of creative writing. Unless one lives in the Monterey area and has read the *Herald* in recent years, *and* bothered to read the poetry section, it is likely that one will not have discovered the wonderful poems of Arthur Porges. To my mind, it is manifestly unfair that this other side to his writing has been languishing in obscurity for so long.

I once asked Arthur why so many of his poems had been published only locally:

"… there are very few markets, and the competition more than fierce, with every top poet in the world sending in stuff."

In the same letter, he went on to discuss some of his favorites:

"I believe that Tennyson's 'Tears, Idle Tears,' is one of the best short poems ever written, just as Keats' 'The Eve of St. Agnes' is one of the best long ones. Kipling wrote some great ballads, but he also had a few subtle, dark poems, little-known but magnificent; and Dante Gabriel Rossetti's 'A Superscription' is a superb sonnet."

Naturally, I was keen to read Arthur's own poetry. Soon after I began corresponding with him he sent me a selection of what he considered to be some of his best poems. These were in the form of newspaper cuttings and original manuscripts. I was intrigued, wanting to read even more. Over the years, thanks to the author himself, I was given the opportunity to read a lot of his poetry; eventually, after inheriting some of his papers when he died, among which were several further poems, I realized I had accumulated a wealth of material. There was certainly enough to put together a bumper collection—should the opportunity to do so ever arise.

Well, as you can see it has now come to pass. Needless to say I am very pleased to be in a position to bring this side to his writing to the attention of a wider audience. Of the poems assembled in this book, most appeared in the aforementioned *Herald*, though some are previously unpublished. Arthur had written a few experimental and light verses in earlier years; I uncovered a few of these and have included an unpublished piece entitled "A Dream." This poem dates from the period just after World War Two when Porges was teaching at the Western Military Academy in Alton, Illinois.

Porges succeeded in selling just two poems to national magazines. "Time-Bomb" appeared in the June 1964 issue of *The Magazine of*

*Fantasy and Science Fiction*. A later, reworked version, "The Real Bomb," is included in this book. His only other sale to a national periodical was "Physics for Fundamentalists," a satirical piece recently published in *Free Inquiry*. A lifelong atheist, Arthur subscribed to this magazine—and also the *Skeptical Inquirer*—for years, describing, with typical humor, the two titles as: "… the only decent magazines for us infidels …" His strong views on religion and his steadfast atheism are on display in several of his poems; readers of this book will be left in no doubt as to where he stood on such matters!

There is a refreshing honesty and clarity of vision in those poems where Porges opines about the random nature of the universe. He firmly believed that we lived in a haphazard world and that all the evidence pointed to the non-existence of a caring, benevolent god looking down upon us. Two explicit examples of this viewpoint are to be found in the poems "Of Ants and Men" and "Foxes—Meet the Hedgehog," both of which express a sentiment I confess to share with the author.

I think it is fair to say that Porges put a lot of himself into many of his poems. Given that he concentrated on poetry, for the most part, in his later years—he was upwards of seventy when the majority of them were written—it's perhaps unsurprising that a large number of his poems deal with such subjects as old age and mortality. His views and, arguably, his preoccupations, certainly come across in such whimsical poems as "On Gravity," "Unwelcome Guests" and "The Years." In these, and others, Arthur often makes use of ancient myths and supernatural elements—to great effect.

As well as drawing on his own thoughts about death, Porges uses the stunning imagery of such poems as "Time's Arrows" to explore his ideas about the nature of time itself and how, in the space of a heartbeat, so much can happen. The contemplation of the inexorable march of time is a recurring motif within his verse.

Other poems are concerned with loss and remembrance. "Fragrance as Memory" is imbued with a delicate poignancy; "Departure" is simple and elegant in its evocation of grief; in "Ah, Maureen!" Porges displays consummate skill in evoking an old man's pure nostalgia for a lost dream of the silver screen. In this latter poem,

Arthur movingly reflects that the dreams of youth are not always lost on the old, that being of an advanced age does not necessarily preclude romantic yearnings—one can still dream.

Aside from the more reflective side to his work, one is continually struck by the imagination and invention evident in such poems as "Foliot" and "Broadcaster." Arthur's poems are nothing if not unique—nobody else writes quite like this! There is much in the way of rare and arcane knowledge inherent throughout his work in this medium. These qualities are demonstrated in "Shadows," wherein Arthur revisits the theme of "The Shadowsmith" (*Fantastic Stories*, September 1960), one of his finest supernatural stories. His verse treatment of this unusual subject is fascinating. It is a meditation upon the differences between shadows, their subtle disparities, their unusual, hidden qualities. He reflects on how we see them, or not, as the case may be, bringing them into focus by engaging our attention through detailed, eloquent descriptions, urging us to "consider shadows." Poems such as these are the products of an open and inquiring mind. For a self-confessed skeptic, Arthur certainly did his research into all manner of "alternative" subjects.

One should bear in mind though, that this is a writer who grew up reading authors such as William Hope Hodgson, H. Rider Haggard, Rudyard Kipling and Arthur Conan Doyle, to name just a few. Porges cut his teeth on fantastic fiction and wrote an awful lot of weird fantasy stories throughout his career. Perhaps inevitably, some of the more off-trail themes he explored in his fiction were carried over into his poetic excursions.

Likewise, as with his fictional output, Arthur makes use of various esoteric subjects and little-known facts for some of his poems. His knowledge and insightful observations of the natural world are conveyed to superb effect in the remarkable "Listener" and "African Food-Chain." His love of classical music comes across in "Saraband" and "Overheard in a Piano Store." And in the brilliant "Captain Jobson," Porges pays homage to an obscure figure from history.

Then there are those poems that are more contemporary in their subject matter. "Executing the Monster" is topical, challenging and quite uncompromising—Arthur pulls no punches here. "Snapshot in

Black-and-White," one of my favorites, carries a fierce anti-racist message. "Six Death Sentences" is an outstanding, almost painfully honest, intense and thought-provoking work. One person I showed it to described it as "amazing."

With such an explosion of ideas and wide range of subjects evident in his poetry, I felt compelled to ask Arthur where he got his inspiration from. I also asked for his thoughts on the process of writing in such a challenging medium:

> "As to writing poetry, yes, it's the hardest of all creative writing, I think. In my case, since I'm not great at lyrics, like Tennyson, but relate to idea-based/dramatic poetry of the sort Browning, Hardy, and Housman wrote, I think of an idea, like the one about the first man to hear a clock tick, and base a poem on that. Or simply a very good line comes to mind, and I build a poem around it. The hard work comes in seeking the exact words, phrases, metaphors and such that are fresh and strong."

Porges' assertion that he was not a lyricist is borne out in a great deal of his poetry. Much of it is indeed very strong on ideas, gleefully unconventional in approach and not overly concerned with meter, rhythm and cadence. But there are at least two poems in this collection that would seem to buck that trend. One notable exception is the incomparable "Spring, 1836," a poem Arthur was very fond of—incidentally, this book is so named in honor of that fact. An understated and charming piece, it depicts a look back into the distant past. In this poem, he shows considerable skill in subtly evoking the poignancy of a certain moment captured in time. The other anomaly in this collection is the evocative "Leaf and Stream," a work of studied beauty that illustrates a lyricism and sensitivity on the part of the author. It is no doubt atypical of Porges' verse output, but is nevertheless heartfelt, affecting and sincere.

There is a core of seriousness, a bristling intensity, to several of his poems. However, Arthur did write a good deal of light verse. I have included some of the best examples of these here. The black humor of "Automatic Pistol" is certainly effective, though maybe a little too dark for some tastes! As an aside, avid readers will perhaps notice a similarity between this and the early story "A Quick Death" (collected in *The Calabash of Coral Island and Other Stories*, 2008). "No Laughing Matter," with its outrageous pun, is also somewhat darkly humorous, but others are delightfully playful and light in tone. These include "Necrology," "Creation and Osculation" (strange titles, these!) and Arthur's lighthearted dedication to a personal friend "To a Dear Lady Born on Midway Island." These poems, and others, aptly showcase Arthur's wit and sense of the absurd.

And I cannot resist giving a special mention to "The News." Of all the humorous verses Porges wrote, I think this one is the most impressive. Again, who else could have written this? It's obviously about Arthur's disaffection with TV news coverage, be it endless updates, self-important anchormen, or just hysterical news reporting in general! This poem has a ring of truth to it. I have a mental picture of Arthur abruptly turning off his television set—after hours of being bombarded with news reports—and feeling impelled to write this piece, inspired by a mixture of wry amusement and irritation. In these lunatic days of round-the-clock bulletins and twenty-four hour news channels, "The News" looks like it will remain relevant for a long time.

There are yet more aspects to Arthur's poetry, but I will leave those for the reader to discover within the pages of this collection. I have so many personal favorites among the poems included here, and I trust all those who buy this book will have fun reading through them all and finding the ones they enjoy most.

I have consciously avoided any attempt to compare his poetry to that of other practitioners—both past and present—of this particular literary discipline. I'm happy to leave such discussions to others; as a devoted Porges fan I am, perhaps, not best placed to act as critic. Nor have I felt the need to highlight his influences, although it's worth noting that he greatly admired the work of the American poet Emily Dickinson (1830-1886), whose unconventional approach doubtless inspired his somewhat idiosyncratic verse style.

Notwithstanding this, Arthur's poems are essentially his own. Moreover I believe that the work on display here, by virtue of its originality, power and honesty, further establishes his reputation as a truly individual author and one deserving of a unique place in the literary firmament. Put simply, poems are an important part of Arthur's legacy.

Well, my shingle is up. It has been a labor of love putting this collection together. But it's also a privilege to honor Arthur's memory in this way by bringing into the light a hitherto unknown—to most, anyway—side to his writing. I think his poems are remarkable and I hope others find much to admire and enjoy in this book.

*Richard Simms*
*Surrey, England*
*October, 2008*

# The Other Smile

You smile, Deirdre:
red wax,
pink membranes,
soft tissues
all retract
to flash enameled bones,
a visual caress,
intimate and tangible
as a lover's kiss,
that exalts my heart.

Something deep inside me,
long frozen,
stirs, thawing briefly.
How I love you, Deirdre!
I, who dare not love you,
knowing that Time,
the insatiable carnivore,
even now nuzzles your body,
claws at your face
lightly, lightly,
talons sheathed;
you are so young, Deirdre.

I dread another smile,
the last, the most private.
No red wax,
no pink membranes,
no soft tissues:
just enameled bones
grinning forever
in the joyless dark.

# Spring, 1836

I found them, quite unexpectedly,
in a dimly-lit alcove
of a magnificent old building,
once a luxury hotel in 1925,
now a shabby but dignified retirement home;
and thought, "How odd!"
There they were, hung on the wall like a painting,
framed, behind glass, in some dark wood,
a narrow column of four butterflies,
titled in an elegant 19th century script,
*Collected in the Spring of 1836.*
Dry, fragile little corpses,
still displaying something of their varied, subtle hues;
and I felt a tiny frisson of grief,
thinking of how these lovely, harmless fliers,
sailing warm April air of a long-gone time,
when a girlish, eager Victoria
was only months from her crown,
sipping nectar from great, glowing blooms,
were snatched from their vague
yet blissful consciousness
and dropped into the deadly fumes of a killing-bottle.
Surely, a few molecules of fragrance
from those flowers, scentless dust
for almost two centuries,
still vibrated in the brittle, faded wings.

# Listener

Barn owl, perched immobile,
lethal talons clench-locked
deep into a rafter's rotting wood,
listening intently, a sentient microphone,
small brain holding no thoughts.
He hears a tuft of moldy straw,
dislodged high up by a prowling rat
wobble hissing through the air
to strike the concrete floor—tick!
Then a mouse scurries along the wall,
seventy grams of timid urgency,
and the bird's great spectral face,
a daunting brown-and-white cameo,
swivels, hidden ears range-finding.
His wings, edged with the softest down,
unfurl without even a whisper of sound;
the killer-claws open,
and the owl takes flight,
dropping noiseless as a shadow
gliding over silk.
Unerringly, he strikes home,
and the mouse's tiny death-squeak
booms like a giant thunderclap.

# Snapshot in Black-and-White

I'm walking down this quiet, sunny street
(very good neighborhood; almost no crime)
minding my own business:
dark suit, white shirt, tie, gleaming shoes,
doggedly upper middle class,
when this elderly white couple
sees me coming, and stops dead,
obviously uneasy, maybe real scared:
(one of *them* on our street? How come?)
So I fix a death's-head grin on my black face,
circle them menacingly twice,
and shout "Boo!"
They jump almost out of their skins,
and I strut by, laughing derisively.
But there is no joy in my assumed mirth,
only more misery and despair,
the latest searing layer.
Sure, my action is stupid, childish,
and worse, futile, changing nothing for the better,
but what the hell will?
I just didn't know what else to do.

# The Corridor

The corridor narrows further here;
my shoulders brush the mildewed walls
that once were pastel-bright.
Surely there was sun-dappling
and meadow-fresh Spring air;
but over a long blur of draining time
the light slowly, imperceptibly dimmed,
and now all four surfaces bleed dusk.
I fear what lies ahead,
but there is no turning back,
now or ever—
the Arrow of Time points one way only.
I see a door on my left,
barely visible in the gloom;
the last was many years ago,
but haunts me still …
When did I begin this strange, harrowing journey?
It must have been as an infant eight decades ago,
but those vague, early dreams are long lost
beyond the farthest outposts of sleep.
And when did I first reach a door in the blank walls?
No doubt of that—on my sixth birthday.
It was small, square, and oddly low,
opening very suddenly to release a little spotted cat
like a toy leopard, that sprang out, hissing and spitting
to claw me viciously, rending my tender flesh.
I awoke whimpering, with the red macules of measles.
"By golly!" Doc Blodgett exclaimed.
"The boy has more rash than skin to hold it!"
Then, when I was fifteen, the second door,
much bigger, wider, and high.
From it there pranced a small dragon,

arrogant in shiny red scales,
leathery bat-wings a spectral display.
Not big enough to breathe flames,
it belched acrid smoke,
and I coughed, long, wrenching paroxysms.
My Scarlet Fever was not severe,
but left me hard of hearing.
There have been many encounters since,
one particularly memorable.
That door was round, of red-brown mottled glass,
set high on the right wall.
It swung open like a porthole
for a giant Promethean vulture
that swooped down, screaming harshly,
to ravage my chest with a scythe-beak
that stabbed agonizingly deep,
piercing flesh and rib-cage to slash my liver.
Hospitalized for weeks, I almost died of hepatitis.
I see this latest door clearly now;
it is close to the dusty carpet,
like a huge mail-slot.
What sort of creature lurks behind it
on this, my eighty-fifth birthday?
Only one I know of, and dread:
a squat, multiclawed scrabbler:
The Crab.
There will be no more doors,
of that I'm very sure.
Not far ahead the Corridor ends,
blank-walled, blindly, in the cold dark.

# Of Ants and Men

A tiny blob of strawberry jam,
overlooked on the table,
and this morning it boiled over
with little red ants.
Annoyed, I flicked dozens to the floor,
where they scuttled off in all directions,
confused and disoriented.
The panicked outriders on the table
could not evade me,
I smashed them singly with my thumbs.
Then I thought,
what if the survivors gathered in a safe corner
down there to discuss the traumatic event?
Why, some would ask guiltily,
were we spared while so many others,
no different in their behavior,
were quickly, ruthlessly crushed?
And, surely, at least one would say,
"It's just His will,
the giant biped god who rules our lives,
and not for us, sinful insects, to question."
And then I had to smile wryly.
Doomed by a smear of jam,
the ants speculate foolishly,
trying to explain the obvious,
that their little lives have no value to their god.
Do we too suffer and die
for such trivial causes, or none at all?
Are we just a kind of ant-life to our god?
Cast a Yeats' cold-eye on a world
perpetually, randomly in extremis,
and deny it if you dare.

# Broadcaster

Behold this young child,
a blind deaf-mute,
horribly deformed,
severely brain-damaged,
curled up, shrunken,
like the near-term fetus of some great beast,
kept alive only by the sterile embrace
of an electromechanical octopus
gripping relentlessly with plastic tentacles.

Yet the encephalograph is not completely flat;
there are odd, intermittent waves,
flickering, bizarre,
with truncated peaks
that would confound Fourier himself;
so somewhere inside this hapless thing
there may be a faint, nightmare consciousness
desperately trying to awake.

But what thoughts are there?
What dreams, badly fragmented,
of yet undiscovered worlds?
What colors never seen by earthly eyes?
What music unheard, unwritten, unsung,
with new harmonies?
What does this little monster broadcast
by means less conceivable
than those being sought by S.E.T.I.
from distant galaxies?
And who will ever receive these frantic transmissions?

# No Laughing Matter

It wasn't Mary's fault.
She's really good-natured for a spotted hyena,
except when I'm late with her meals,
but road-kill just isn't predictable.
Great sense of humor, too;
even as a cub she always laughed at my jokes.
But Dad is pissed off at both of us:
"When I gave her to you as a pet—
it was your tenth birthday, remember—
you were supposed to control her,
and now she's killed and eaten my only daughter,
bones and all, right there in the yard;
that's a bit much, son."
I explained that Grace shouldn't have teased her,
but my kid sister has always been a brat.
Anyhow, when she jeered at Mary,
imitating her high-pitched laugh,
it's no wonder the dumb brute lost it.
Sure, I was wrong, the way I reacted,
but Dad didn't make a fuss until I joked—
how could I resist such a great pun?—
"Hail Mary, full of Grace!"

# Connections

On January 14, 1804,
some rich ore was dug out by Nathan Davis.
It was then smelted and refined by Hiram Wells.
Melted once more, and carefully spilled
from the wooden tower, the stream separated,
as it fell, into hundreds of near-perfect spheres,
the operation being supervised by Peter Wainwright.
One of the shiny lead balls, exactly like its fellows,
had a unique, terrible destiny:
fired from an elegant dueling pistol by Aaron Burr,
it mortally wounded the Golden Boy
of the new republic,
        Alexander Hamilton …

On January 14, 1865,
ore was extracted from the same mine
by Walter Perkins.
It was then smelted and purified by Joseph Kelly.
Remelted, and spilled from the old wooden tower,
the operation monitored by Samuel Wainwright,
grandson of Peter, the shower of liquid metal
again produced hundreds of spheres.
One of the gleaming balls, exactly like its fellows,
had a unique, tragic destiny:
fired from a small, chunky Derringer
by John Wilkes Booth,
it fatally wounded the 16th President
of the United States,
        Abraham Lincoln.

# Bishop Paul's Vision

I know exactly what you're planning, Lord.
You gave us another chance after the flood,
but we hardened our hearts and again chose evil.
Now we have sinned beyond redemption,
a loathsome skin-disease of the pristine world,
leprous-white here and in Europe;
gangrenous-black in Africa;
scabrous-yellow in Asia.
Last night I had an unbearable vision:
You pressed one mighty finger against the earth,
instantly stopping its rotation.
The blocked energy raged into million-degree heat;
the towering Himalayan peaks slumped,
melting like giant piles of sugar;
the deep waters boiled miles-high,
violently sweeping away the slag of dead cities.
London, New York, Paris, Rome, Moscow,
all steaming plains of utter desolation,
and when I lifted my eyes to beg your divine mercy,
I saw the four great nightsuns of Orion:
Betelgeuse, Bellatrix, Rigel, and Saiph
tumbling headlong from the black vault.

# Shadows

I

Consider shadows:
truly, uniquely two-dimensional,
weightless, soundless, inhumanly supple
in a crass world dominated by clunky solids;
infinitely varied, multicolored
as cast by wood-fires, table-lamps,
spotlights that probe with white fingers,
and scattered bulbs that dabble obscurely in penumbras,
but above all the great yellow sun,
the ultimate shadow-master.

Consider shadows:
and what they fall upon:
grass, wood, snow, stone, water,
and countless other surfaces.
Add the daunting complexities of projective geometry,
how a shadow may be thrown from any angle,
by different intensities and hues of light,
able to vault swiftly or glide smoothly
from one configuration to another,
from the amorphous black pool
when the sun blazes down from his zenith
to a greatly-extended image at dusk.
If in tandem with one special person,
it must bend deftly over a curb with never a wrinkle,
or effortlessly scale a high wall.
A shadow on rough, grey concrete
is related only distantly,
when cast by powerful halogens
to one flickering by candle

on polished hardwood.
Then there's the blue-black splotch,
strangely corrugated,
on Polar ice under the Midnight Sun,
or the most demanding possible performance
that can be expected of a shadow,
made by gauzy silver moonlight,
when scudding clouds and shivering leaves
shatter the Dark Others to gyrating flecks.

Consider shadows …

II

My shadow has aged right along with me,
for eight busy decades perfectly in step,
whenever the light permitted;
yet only with this somber sunset
did I really notice its sad deterioration.
Just as I am frail, stoop-shouldered, and unsteady,
shambling cautiously along the cracked sidewalk,
warily alert for dangerous foot-trippers,
so my meager shadow bends and totters behind me.
But this evening it is no longer alone;
it has been joined by another dark shape,
much bigger, with the likeness of a coach,
drawn overhead, how I cannot say,
by a team of vaguely equine beasts.
Who would have expected Time's winged chariot
to cast so black and lusterless a shadow?

# Overheard in a Piano Store

All our pianos are choice.
Look: Bechsteins, Bosendorfers, Steinways—
names that ring like silver trumpets.
A family business since 1800.
That one, with no name?
Seems out of place, yes?
Small, a bit shabby even.
My firm made it in 1852.
Just listen to its tone—
how it sings!
(Remind you of anyone?)
It's the soundboard,
the soul of the piano.
Still the original,
aged and mellowed like a Strad.
It came from an old spruce
that grew in Potter's Field,
one with a famous lost grave
that somehow nourished the tree.
This piano is glorified by that,
music from a handful of dust—
the dust of Mozart.

*Note: Mozart died in 1791, and his body put in a pauper's grave, location unknown.*

# The Years

Now is the time of waiting,
not as the blind hemisphere awaits the dawn,
or a yearning seed the reveille of April,
but as the savaged deer, windbroken,
fronts the slavering wolves.

The infant's earliest steps
are on the incline dipping to the tomb,
but so gradual is that first slope
he does not realize that every path goes down,
each moment a point of no return;
nor can the stealthy footbeat of pursuing years
be heard above the silver bugles of youth.

But, at eighty,
when a winter freeze cracks my bones,
and an icy rain mutters of mortality,
then the marching of the years
outdrums the mighty clamor of the world,
drowns the bloodsong in the veins,
and even stills the pulse of love.

# Foxes—Meet the Hedgehog

Theologians are foxes,
knowing many things:
Why poor Job got it in the neck;
why those dissolute clowns in Sodom
carried on as if there were no Gomorrah;
why innocent little kids
are always dying horribly,
while the wicked flourish
like the Green Bay Packers;
what God really expects of us,
and why He so rarely gets it;
but they can't explain any of it
well or even plausibly.

Now I am a hedgehog,
knowing only one big thing,
but with absolute certainty
and overwhelming evidence:
That Life is a tale told by an idiot,
full of sound and fury,
signifying nothing,
nada, zilch, zero,
especially a caring God
who gives one little damn.

# Foliot

My grave has been lost for six centuries;
its modest stone, bearing a cryptic symbol,
a little bar with pallets, gradually tilted,
then sank, very slowly, deep into the loam,
later sown with rye, of my native Bavaria,
but my enduring monuments are everywhere.

For I contrived the foliot,
fitting it to the crown wheel just so;
no room for error, a perfect interplay,
a complex symphony of moving parts.
Then I wound the thick rope
on the wooden cylinder,
raising the massive iron weight—
and stared, heart racing like a lover's at climax.
Were those new, unique pallets suitably designed,
able to lock a single tooth of the cogwheel,
while crisply freeing the next?

Yes! Yes! Dei gratia: the escapement came alive,
paused—this was the pregnant caesura—
and moved again with marvelous vigor,
a wonderful stammer, never before audible.
My bits of brass, so ingeniously made,
had finally tamed unruly Time
that fleered at mute sandglasses,
erratic, dripping clepsydras,
and whirring fan-flys.
I heard the faint staccato beat,
a cry like that of a newborn babe—
I, Walther Reichardt,
the first man for whom a clock ticked.

# The News

The News! The News!
The daily News!
A spate, a torrent of endless blather;
Brokaw, Jennings, Blitzer, Rather!
The News! The News!
It's rarely new,
its fresh insights very few!
The News! The News!
The rehashed News!
Arabs and Jews!
Bedouwins and Druse!
Ten murders—No Clues!
The News! The News!
The Refried News!
Record Price for Famous Greuze!
His Mistress Sues!
The Niners Lose!
The News! The News!
Driving and Booze!
The Latest in Zoos!
The News! The News!
The Drumbeat of News!
How those Anchors jaw!
Can't somebody silence Bernard Shaw?
The News! The News!
The overkilled News!
We're drowning under wordy ooze!
Please, no more; my ears are sore!
End the terror of an hour with Lehrer!
The News! The News! Often so old;
seldom hot, but rather cold!
A pox on each medium;

let's stop the tedium
of the News! The News!
It makes us snore;
even worse than Al the Bore!
I suffer from the Network Blues—
let's have a moratorium on News!

# Creation and Osculation

When Adam and Eve were made by God,
one small mistake was rather odd:
he gave them each a central nose—
why such a goof, do you suppose?
When two young lovers try to kiss,
a nasal clash is hard to miss!
Had I been God when life began,
I would have made a better plan.
All noses to the right would bend,
and lovers' faces neatly blend,
so when the couple joined their lips,
no tilts, no twists, just tender sips!

# A Dream of Judgment

In my dream I faced the Last Judgment,
bleakly aware of a constricted, loveless life.
"You were always cold-hearted, selfish," the Judge
said, "using money and gifts instead of caring. Never
once did you tell anybody, 'I love you.' "

I hung my head, not daring to speak the truth,
that the phrase was too cryptic and potent for me.

Then the Judge studied the record again, and said,
"Ah, I was wrong.
Just once, when your aunt,
who raised you with much affection and laughter
when your parents died,
was on her deathbed far away,
you phoned her and choked out the words,
knowing you lied, not having the emotion for real,
'I love you, Fran.' "

He looked at me with mournful eyes, was silent briefly,
then said, "That alone redeems you; it is enough.
Welcome to Heaven."

And I awoke, sobbing …

# Automatic Pistol

I rest on the bedside table
thinking metallic thoughts.
I yearn to fire again;
it has been years,
and only at targets,
bottles, cold bloodless things.
I want to kill something;
I need to kill something,
to let my hammer fall,
driving the pin forward
to strike the testy primer,
exploding the powder …
The lead slug,
deadly child of my steel womb,
flies down the grooved barrel,
rotating, rubbing, growing hot
(how good that feels!)
Then birth:
My child free for a brief, violent life.
900 feet per second,
able to shatter bones.
Oh, for an intruder!

# Stone

Out on a random cross-country walk,
I found this really big, jagged stone,
half-buried, alone in an arid field.
Feeling oddly puckish, very atypical for me,
I rapped on it vigorously with a smaller one:
      Hey, rock!
      (Silence)
I struck it again, harder:
      Hey there, rock!
      (Silence)
Then, for a third time, I really slammed it:
      Hey you, rock!
And it spoke to me
in a voice unlike any I've ever heard:
      Go away!
      I'll be marking your grave soon enough.

# Effie Warvelle
# at the River Styx

Sixty-five years ago she was a tiny wavelet
on the great, tranquil pond of Academia.
Effie Warvelle was teaching English Literature
from Beowulf to Dickens
in a small, inner-city college
with not one square foot of campus,
an institution undistinguished as herself.
She had thoroughly mastered, even memorized,
much of the canon,
and obviously delighted in it.
As a student there for one quarter,
I knew nothing of her own education and private life,
that fluffy, ribbony, fastidious little woman,
but her subtle insights and radiant spirit impressed me.
She always began each session in exactly the same way
with "Good Morning—Game is called,"
in a bright, chirpy, musical chant.
I never quite understood that phraseology,
its context or source in literature,
but we all knew it meant for us to settle down,
notebooks at the ready, for the day's lesson,
perhaps for some witty, shocking candor
in her faintly British accent
about the bawdy Restoration comedies,
for in our time Freud was the God/Devil of the Arts.
Now, over six decades later,
I still wonder when and how the Dark Angel, Azrael,
summoned Charon to lead Effie, very gently, I hope,
to his black boat swaying in the Styx,
where I can't help thinking

that in proper English Lit mode,
handing over the mandatory obolus for her fare,
she declaimed, still chirpy and bright,
"Come, lovely and soothing death—
you are but a groom which brings a taper
to the outward room: Game is called."

# Sappho's Lover Speaks
**(After the Greek)**

Stay away from my grave, red-haired woman.
Alive, I could never get enough of you;
my want was deeper and darker than this black pit
where I lie alone and lonely.
If your pale, narrow foot I love to kiss
bends even one blade of grass overhead,
on this, my first night without you,
I might claw through the heavy loam,
April-sweet with Spring rain,
seeking one last glimpse of your face
before old Charon dips his oars
to bear me away forever.

# Two Wrynesses

Donned repeatedly while they last,
there are countless favorite
hats, shirts, neckties, pants, and shoes.
There are beloved
jackets, dresses, skirts, nylons, and heels.
And then, finally, Death,
the lusterless black cloak
worn only once.

Absolutely,
there are no Absolutes.
Kind deeds are tinged with subtle malice,
and where blackest evil breaks a slimy trail,
some small flowers may star the tainted soil.
One twitch of a single molecule
shatters the myth of Absolute Zero,
and the deepest silence,
even that of a long-abandoned grave
rings constantly with tiny sounds.

# Executing the Monster

Two days ago they executed Walter Hobart Payne,
The Monster.
It seemed a sadly familiar sort of crime:
a quiet loner, considered harmless, if odd,
polite and pleasant to his neighbors,
but reclusive, reticent, with few if any close friends;
just a competent, grey bean-counter at the office,
who suddenly, for no apparent reason,
buys a 12-gauge shotgun,
charges into a kindergarten,
and blasts away right and left,
killing nine children,
wounding eighteen more
(three will be in wheelchairs for life)
plus the popular young teacher.

I was the prosecutor;
my first really big case,
and did I ever demonize the guy!
The defense did its best, trying hard,
calling several witnesses,
people who knew him years ago as a kid.
They spewed the usual googoo excuses:
horribly abused as a child:
beaten, starved, molested,
but, of course, nobody cared,
not with so many dead little innocents.

I was ruthless, implacable, wanting him erased,
hammering hard about individual responsibility.
Payne knew exactly what he was doing,
knew right from wrong, but deliberately chose evil.

He sat there in court, passive, indifferent, blankfaced,
never showing a scintilla of remorse,
while the grieving, distraught parents
glared their molten hatred at him.
It took the jury only eighty minutes:
guilty, with special circumstances,
a guaranteed death penalty in this state.

Then, yesterday, at the autopsy, a surprise—
a giant brain-tumor, right near the optic nerve;
(Payne would soon have been blind.)
So that was the real Monster,
totally malignant, unlike him.
It was what sent him charging into that kindergarten,
not any murderous choice of his own, the poor slob.

Know something?
Today I'd like to die myself.

# Departure

My mother would never say, "Goodbye."
It was too bleak and final for her.
Instead, in a comically bad accent for each,
it was always one of these:
"Au revoir,
"Auf Wiedersehen,
"Adios,
"Ciao,"
or even in the plummiest British,
"Parting is such sweet sorrow …"

But then, at her sixty-first birthday party,
in the middle of a sentence,
she suddenly sat back in her chair,
her big, brown eyes,
soft and warm as melted caramel,
closed, and she said very quietly,
"Goodbye, my Darlings,"
and left us forever.

# The Amazonian Mail

In Amazonia,
a stamp costs two draks;
with it,
you can send a one-ounce letter
to any part of the country,
which seems a great bargain,
since there are ninety draks to the dollar.

But—
This huge stamp,
with its profile of El Supremo,
weighs exactly one ounce,
so all mail in Amazonia
is returned to the sender,
marked, "Insufficient Postage."

Once, a man, desperate to correspond,
wrote "Hi!" on a stamp,
and mailed it to a friend,
but it still came back,
marked, "Insufficient Postage."

The man sued, and lost;
the Chief Justice ruled:
"Even though the official scales
are not sensitive enough to weigh the ink in 'Hi!'
it is logically obvious that even a single period
must increase the weight to more than an ounce."
So all mail, even solo stamps,
was returned to the sender,
marked, "Insufficient Postage."

Last week, an ingenious woman
wrote a long letter to a friend,
but addressed it to herself,
putting the friend's address
on the upper left-hand corner.

In Amazonia,
all mail is returned to the sender,
stamped, "Insufficient Postage."

      AHA!


# Physics for Fundamentalists


No, not Armageddon: too slow and bloody.
As Einstein taught us,
when matter and antimatter engage,
there is instantaneous, total, mutual annihilation,
a gigantic burst of atomic energy.
Well, in His Second Coming,
when Christ finally confronts the Antichrist,
Jesus, being what He always was,
will lovingly embrace his Dark Antagonist,
a combined mass of 130 kilograms—
      BOOM!
And the world ends.

# The Sounds of Death

My hearing is unique in this world.
When I choose, I can hear the exact microsecond
as Life ends and Death strikes home,
a subtly different sound in each case,
but basically the same for a given species.

When an insect dies, snapped up by a lizard,
there is a sharp little click.
A mouse, pierced by the talons of a hawk,
makes a faint metallic ping,
and a zebra, drawing its last agonized breath
in the suffocating clamp of a lion's jaws,
sounds like the off-key clang of a cracked bell.

Humans all perish to music,
some of it harsh and discordant, ugly,
most reasonably harmonious and poignant,
like that of familiar composers;
but when my dearest wife died suddenly,
I heard a great chord of transcendent beauty
no earthly hand could ever have written,
and no musical instrument will ever play …

# Time's Arrows

The old clock, austerely elegant,
eight feet of burnished mahogany,
has stood for over a century
at the foot of the spiral staircase,
itself a miracle of airy architecture,
confining space in its graceful twist,
evoking the vital helix of DNA.

The clock's deep sonorous beats
as the long mercury-compensated pendulum
sways majestically up and back,
are like tiny sonic booms
in the dusky purple stillness,
counting out lives by potent seconds.

Outside in the flower-drenched garden,
the mossy sundial, even older,
tells a grim truth by inscription:
It is later than you think.

And just as no princes, powers, or learned doctors
can drive the gnomon's shadow counterclockwise,
neither can they reverse one magisterial Tock
into the preceding Tick.

The old clock obeys only Time,
always loosing arrows that fly one way—
            forever.

# The Worm Turns

They who had so long terrorized me,
monsters of many haunted nights in bed,
now fled from me like ants under a poison spray.
Exultant, I pursued and harried them.
I flung one hairy, amorphous thing right over a house,
then charged into a huddle of foul beasts,
punching, kicking, even fragmenting them;
and when one snarling abomination, vaguely canine,
blocked my path, all a-bristle,
I booted it into the gutter.
A skeleton, a familiar apparition from past nightmares,
tried to get away, but was much too slow.
I easily overtook the clacking creature,
smashed its rib-cage with vicious blows,
scattered the dry bones,
and stamped them into powder.
Then, laughing, I uprooted a massive iron fence,
and with it flailed a mob of cowering ghouls
(how unsubstantial they seemed!)
and a towering goblin, fire-eyed,
with teeth like glass splinters,
cringing under my metal scourge,
wailed in a thick, bestial voice,
"It's no use—he's fearless and invulnerable now—
he knows he's dreaming!"
With one mighty roundhouse blow
I shattered its spectral head—
and awoke,
still shaking with malicious glee.

# Immortality

It's known that all living things must die
whether stupid or very clever
so it's wise to cast a cold eye
on just how that fruitcake lives forever!
Yes, I will perish, whatever my endeavor;
tell me, how does simple fruitcake live forever?
Archimedes proved he could move the
earth with a lever but he's gone for eons,
while fruitcake is forever!
It moves around from home to home;
from pole to pole it's free to roam
but always whole and never hacked
ever denser and more compact.
There will never be an end to fruitcake glut
since nary a one is ever cut.
No fruitcake's life is ever done
and some insist there's only one!
Truly, it defines "eternal"
this dessert some call infernal.
If we could only find its gene
say, wouldn't that be peachy-keen?
The greatest discovery that ever was,
and we might live forever, as the fruitcake does!

# Captain Jobson

Surely all his sins may be forgiven
this English Captain Jobson,
whom I see clearly,
even across the gulf of centuries.
A whilom rogue, lecher, thief;
perhaps a casual killer,
but never in cold blood.
Plaguey hot as mustard,
as befitted a bold corsair
of the devious First Elizabeth;
full of choler, and Damn Your Eyes, Sir!
Nothing chill and passive;
devilish quick to smite a careless helmsman,
or to cleave a dark Castilian head
in some desperate cut-and-thrust
on the canted deck of a treasure galleon;
but not a discounter of souls;
no man-buyer, he.
The trumpets must have sounded for him
on the Other Side;
silver trumpets jubilating together,
welcoming Captain Jobson,
who would not deal in slaves.
Surely the great trumpets blared,
or else Heaven's a cruel lie,
and laughter rang in Hell.

*Note: In 1623, a Captain Jobson refused to buy black women slaves offered by a Mandingo trader, saying, "... we were a people who did not deal in any such commodities ..."*

# A Red Dawn

After the horrendous war of 2047,
nuclear, biochemical, and world-wide,
nothing moved or grew anywhere,
except, maybe in the lightless abyss
of the Mariana Trench,
36,000 feet beneath the Pacific,
and in a few massive underground shelters,
where a handful of humans still survived,
eating devitalised, packaged food,
greyfaced, wasted, rarely smiling,
full of unrelenting despair,
until one morning in 2062
a woman drearily opening corroded cans
for a scant, savorless daily meal,
suddenly burst into joyous tears
over her stained, worn table
to find it suddenly boiling with tiny red ants.

# The Invitation

Two entities, invisible, intangible,
endlessly patient, vigilant, opportunists,
long-time partners in a deadly game,
watching her intently, anticipating greedily:
She is sixteen today.

"There," says one, "her first cigarette!
I expected it sooner: twelve, fourteen,
even at nine, but no matter;
it's my invitation at last;
now I can invade her."

And the squat thing, vaguely crablike,
scrabbles soundlessly towards the girl,
serrated pincers working viciously.
Then, to his spectral companion:
"I'll see you later, as usual."

The skeletal shape nods a fleshless skull,
indifferent to Time,
knowing centuries
only as tiny chips of eternity.
A grey finger-bone strokes sharp metal,
then he shoulders his scythe,
and strides off to an immediate appointment.

# To a Dear Lady
# Born on Midway Island

Your relatives on Midway, that "tiny spot,"
are truly a bizarre and eccentric lot;
although some are mammals, quite a few are not.
All those shiny scales and thick, glossy furs,
moving so fast—like you!—they are often blurs.
Clumsy boobies that swoop down and crash-land,
multi-limbed creatures that pop from the sand;
fine feathers and fins,
and such oily skins;
lots of whiskers and powerful flippers,
waterproof coats without any zippers;
sleek dolphins all frolic,
stingrays diabolic,
my little hummingbird, how can it be true
that these strange creatures are related to you?
Yes, many are survivors, in Life's Battle winners,
but what a tough bunch to round up
for holiday dinners!

# A Satire of Circumstance

**(After Thomas Hardy)**

My father, that kind and selfless man,
lay in his bedroom, slowly dying;
I could hear each rasping, hard-won breath
as I sat, racked by sick despair,
in the tiny, cluttered kitchen,
the winter sun not yet risen,
hoping for the impossible,
a quicker, easier death,
when, from the next apartment,
came the smell of frying bacon.
My olfactory bulb went wild,
instantly overpowering the cognitive;
warm saliva flooded my mouth,
and after a tense, all-night vigil,
I was ravenously hungry.
Damn the treacherous glands
so arrogantly taking over,
and in a single explosive microsecond
blotting out months of grieving!
In the name of God, how could bacon frying
make me forget that my father was dying?

# A Dream

I dreamed a great dead star
came hurtling from the black of empty space.
Ten thousand sunless worlds adrift in night
had seen it pass and warmed it not.
First-born of the heavens, frozen to the heart
and Earthward bound, sweeping a pathway
through the burning dust of lesser stars,
it filled the moonlit sky.

I took a parting look at Earth,
all warm and green with Spring,
and felt a doubt—the very first.
But then I looked again with clearer gaze
and hid my eyes, ashudder at the sight.

I could have stayed the rushing doom.
My hand alone had power
to wrench it from its ordained course
before the moon that stood between
was flung a spray of silver tears across the night.

Instead, like warmest greeting
to a long-awaited friend,
I cried: "It's time you came!"
And waited smiling for the end.

# Survivor

It survives for centuries,
naked in the soil,
or deep in the corrosive sea.
It survives massacres
in Bosnia,
in Rwanda,
in South America by death squads.

Mere flesh softens,
liquefies,
vaporizes noisomely.
Small bones crumble away,
pulvis et nihil,
but It survives,
a tough, hard guardian
of a vital, squishy pudding.

It survives anatomy classes,
even autopsies.
It survives all these and more.
Sometimes its fleshless, gaping jaws
scream silently,
miming fear and outrage,
but more often it just grins maliciously
in macabre triumph,
the ultimate survivor—
      The Skull.

# Unwelcome Guests

To me, at eighty,
and in failing health,
he's not much better
than his older brother.
Neither is welcome in my home;
you never know how they'll behave.
But there's nothing I can do
about their visits;
they just show up,
one daily, often bringing something
I'd rather not have.
The other, only once,
(but he's really obnoxious)
usually without notice:
Old Mr. Death and his capricious junior
named Tomorrow.

# Apple

I lie here on the damp English ground
among dozens of my fellows
that like me dropped from the old tree.
My skin is beginning to wrinkle,
and fermentation is well under way,
since wasps, ever the topers,
are testing me for alcohol.
Soon I'll be shriveled and moldy,
but I am not like those others:
I am unique, destined to be immortal—
three days ago Newton saw me fall.

# The Real Bomb

This is the bomb
that dooms us all;
made my Mom,
pear-shaped, small.
No fission
no fusion,
no MC square:
just starving kids,
world-cupboard bare.
Presenting The Womb—
        BOOM!

# Six Death Sentences

Eleanor Herrick, forty-eight:
she thinks about the people on Death Row,
and weeps, just a little, quietly,
for she is strong and self-contained.

Kwami Stedman, thirty:
he killed a cop in cold blood four years ago;
three shots in the back,
but is still very much alive after six appeals,
eating wolfishly, sleeping well,
watching cable TV.

Harry Emerson, fifty-one:
he kidnapped, tortured, murdered
a seven-year-old girl in 1988.
He enjoys his Playboys,
studies law books,
pumps iron while thinking up petitions.

Luis Vasquez, thirty-six:
he stabbed his pregnant wife to death.
That was ten years ago,
but thanks to repeated stays
he's alive, well, has gained sixty pounds.

The Mendoza twin sisters, nineteen:
they poisoned their wealthy parents in 1993,
but have so far escaped execution,
once by only four hours.
They claim to have found Christ
and been born again, new and guilt-free.

Eleanor Herrick envies all five.
She got her death sentence decades ago
from too much hot summer sun,
but it was just confirmed by Dr. Mason.
Pressed, he gravely gave her four months.
Malignant melanoma; metastasized; hopeless.
She appeals daily, in silence,
to Somebody, Anybody, maybe Up There,
but has not received even one Stay of Execution.

# The Little Republic
# of Uforia

Uforia's only law is do no harm;
make your peaceful way through wit and charm.
Its population of just one million and three
believes basic civility the vital key.
The only person ever struck by a fist
had freely signed a release as a masochist.
There's only one lawyer, a lonely soul,
who lives on his relatives and the dole.
His legal knowledge is very stale;
to face a jury would turn him pale,
but he cheerfully does the best he can,
sharing a room with the Maytag man.
Sadly, there's no Uforia on the map,
but we surely could use one to fill the gap.

# Saraband

This is no place for such music,
so haunting a rhythm,
evoking summer nights
in the gardens of Spain.
There are no majas down here,
and no nightingales;
only rusty, weed-blurred steel,
the remains of a crumpled hold—
the shattered forepart of the *Sussex*,
blasted away from the main vessel,
now half buried in grey silt
under the turbulent English Channel.
The relic of a forgotten tragedy,
resting in perpetual darkness
for over eighty unremembered years.

But listen—
a faint, tympanic beat,
like that of a stately dance,
surely, a saraband,
percussively played by white bones
that nod, curtsey, and twirl
in the chill dark,
in the tiny surges
born of the mad waves far above,
exchanging staccato kisses.
The bones of Enrique Granados,
castanets of the dead.

*Note: The great Spanish composer, Enrique Granados, along with his wife, drowned when the* Sussex *was torpedoed by a German submarine in 1916.*

# Smashing the Mirror

Heard the news about Rufus Herrick?
You know, the young billionaire.
Well, it turns out that eighteen years ago
he secretly bought a small island
way off in the Pacific, set up a lab,
hired a few biotech whizzes,
and had himself cloned.
Ever since, he's raised the kid,
teaching him all he knows,
which is how to get money and clout.
Then, last night, they had one terrible fight;
the servants saw the whole thing.
Herrick was screaming at the boy,
calling him ungrateful, selfish, arrogant,
loving nobody but himself,
a real young monster.
"How I loathe you!" he jowls;
but the clone just laughs, jeering,
"Of course—I'm a living mirror,
and you can't stand your reflection.
Nice going, Older Brother."
Then he gets sorta biblical:
"To really know thyself, know thy clone."
Well, that drove Herrick nuts.
He rushes out, comes back with his gun,
practically foaming at the mouth,
blows the kid away, and then himself.
Hey, isn't that like killing yourself twice?

# African Food-Chain

Hundreds of zebras stolidly grazing,
a slow, random diffusion of stripes,
almost fluorescent under a dagger sun.
If panicked into flight,
they quickly become a giant stream,
racing across the hot plain,
in chaotic eddies of black-and-white,
swirls difficult for a predator to attack.

Immobile, crouching low in the tall grass,
a lion watches intently, and waits,
looking for a single, vulnerable target:
a sick or disabled adult; even better, a calf
with small, harmless hooves, a little apart,
to one side of the confusing herd.

When he finds one, he will charge,
moving with awesome speed and power,
great humps of shoulder-muscle flexing,
to seize his prey by the throat,
suffocating it in moments.

But what is the consciousness of a zebra?
It has little of the lion's intelligence.
How aware is this passive herbivore?
Maybe it knows a vague kind of beastly self,
but surely not the real truth,
which is essentially metaphysical,
that it is only a machine for turning grass into zebra,
and zebra meat into lion.

Even the lion doesn't know that,
nor the hovering vulture
that will claim them both at the end …


# Incident


When the Quake of the Century
struck without warning,
driving rivers over their banks,
leveling thousands of massive structures,
splitting vast acres of dry land
like skin under a savage flogging,
in the Grand Canyon of the Colorado,
a high cliff shuddered
like a great beast with ague,
and a Bighorn sheep,
for the first time ever,
lost its footing,
to fall five hundred feet
and dye ancient red rocks
a brighter, smoking scarlet.

# The Bridge

Again the bad dream:
I am lost, far from home,
in the most dangerous part of town,
with the sun setting.
Even when I know the way back,
rarely the case, and never for sure,
there are always daunting obstacles:
an unbelievably vast construction ditch,
never finished, miles long,
far too deep to cross,
impossible to bypass before dark;
freeways swarming with fast cars;
high cyclone fences topped with barbed wire;
endless, slow freight trains
with countless clacking flatcars;
and close-set, tacky houses,
unlit, sagging, and unpainted.
If I do find a narrow path between them
after a long, anxious search,
it invariably leads to cluttered yards
where snarling dogs keep guard
and often inflict bloody, agonizing bites.
The shabby streets are Stygian;
furtive figures, many grotesque,
barely human in shape, drift past me.
I plead with taciturn strangers,
almost invisible in the murk—
which way is home, please?
But most ignore me with never a word,
shuffling by hastily.
Finally, one pauses to say
in a thick, almost incomprehensible voice:

"There is a deep ravine ahead,
with a long bridge across it,
but it's hard to find …"
He gestures vaguely,
soon dislimbing in the gloom.
I quicken my pace, longing desperately to be home,
and see the bridge, dead ahead.
It is crank and obviously hazardous,
but I risk it gladly in great strides,
caring little about the absence of guardrails,
the raging water over fanged rocks below,
driven by much greater fears, and then awake—
oh, the joy of that awakening!—
safe in my own bed.
But I am sure, not knowing why,
that some night soon
I'll be on the wrong side again—
and the bridge will be down.

# How the World Will End

No—
not by fire, ice, asteroid, plague,
or the Wrath of God.
Rather, all businesses will cease to operate;
nothing will be made or sold;
no parks or playgrounds will be open;
no public activities will survive,
all for fear of ruinous lawsuits,
and millions of desperate, starving lawyers
will rampage all over the world
in a blind fury about nobody left to sue,
giving the quietus to the civilization
they so greedily ravaged.

# Necrology

So many strange deaths in my family …
My father, tending roses in his garden,
was suddenly infested by aphids;
we sprayed him immediately,
but he soon expired …
My poor mother then got the seven-year-itch,
and scratched herself away in tiny, white flakes,
like a miniature dandruff blizzard,
down to a fragile forty pounds.
She then slipped between the bars
of a sewer grating in the street,
and was flushed seaward,
never to be seen again …
My brother, surfing in Monterey Bay,
was pecked to death by grebes,
and his young widow,
grebe-stricken,
piled up six Sunday newspapers,
jumping from the stack to her death.
What will my own fate be,
I, the last of this doomed family?
My neighbor's pet hyena,
a great, surly brute,
laughs meaningly
as I pass the sagging fence …

# The Shield

My friend, the cynical poet,
who, gifted with a stone-cold Yeatsian Eye,
has completely banished all his darker emotions,
explains:
"Shakespeare got it exactly right
in just one loaded sentence
that negated all the fatuous theology forever:
     'Life is a tale told by an idiot,
      full of sound and fury,
      signifying nothing.'
Once you accept that iron truth unreservedly,
you'll be free, never to wonder or question again,
but just try for the life you really want,
fully aware you may not get it,
and that realization will guarantee absolutely
that you'll never have to grieve over anybody again."

# Taking the
# More-Traveled Road

I'm on my way to Thanatopolis,
Capitol City of Oblivion.
I don't know which road I'm on,
or even where that shadow-city is,
but there are countless routes,
long, short, broad, narrow,
going uphill or down,
dark, well-lighted, rough, smooth,
thronged or deserted.
One hears of tortuous detours,
but they only delay the traveler;
nobody ever bypasses Thanatopolis,
although I welcome them,
fearing the end of my journey.
But there is no stopping,
and it doesn't really matter,
even if my feet box the compass.
You can't possibly miss Thanatopolis;
the most careless traveler cannot miss it.

# On Gravity

Although my most malign foes are diseases,
I am obsessed by Gravity, called a weak force,
which makes me smile wryly.
It often felled me as a toddler,
yet I never feared it then,
but, tumbling to the floor,
joined in my parents' laughter.
I scorned it as a vigorous, sure-footed youth,
except when it brought my flung ball to earth
sooner than my teen arrogance expected.
But now, at eighty,
I anxiously scan what's underfoot:
wet, slick asphalt;
deep-fissured concrete;
an ominous smear of motor oil,
and I beware of Gravity,
knowing that some day soon
the ground will rise up suddenly
to strike me down, and Gravity will,
as it always does, win the game
by breaking my old bones
and dispatching me posthaste
first to a hospital bed,
and then to the Black Gulf of Nil—
a powerful, lethal blow by a weak force.

# Time Gap

Between one moment and the next,
a tiny gap in Time,
yet an irretrievable void
far greater than those dividing galaxies—
so much so terrible can happen:
      a heart stops;
      an artery bursts in a brain;
      a bullet brings instant death;
      a giant meteor splits the earth.
So between tick! and tock!
she died.
The sky fell;
my world collapsed,
but Time's Arrow
flew on,
forever irreversible,
and the grave gulped her.

# Ah, Maureen!

The old man is gaunt, deeply-wrinkled, very frail;
his arthritic, red-knuckled hands
seem too big for such thin wrists;
the vertical muscles in his turkey-neck are taut cables;
as a bartender's ominous quip puts it,
"The snakes are out!"

He is watching the young Errol Flynn,
incredibly handsome, dashing, athletic, debonair,
at large on a gaudy pirate ship,
courting a flame-haired, lissom beauty,
all flashing eyes, red lips, saucy cleavage,
that quintessential Hollywood colleen,
Maureen O'Hara at her peak loveliness.

Yes, the old man has known a few devoted women,
but none like this enchantress of the lilting voice.
They were never what he really wanted,
offering an indescribable, bodiless exaltation,
unattainable by mortals, but reserved for gods,
a union enjoyed by Oberon and Titania, perhaps,
barely hinted at by the absurd,
florid novels of his youth.

Even now, eight decades later,
he has deep, inexpressible yearnings
that never could be satisfied in this world,
but he'd gladly trade all his juiceless years
for one glorious hour as a gallant young swordsman
on a fantasy pirate ship, gaily wooing a pert Irish miss.

# A Promise

Being very old,
and on Final Notice,
I say to my young friend
(no, she is far more than that,
although I dare not tell her,
since Time's barbed arrow
which pierced my heart,
only grazed her,
so six irreversible decades
forever divide us)
the amateur astronomer:
"In about twenty years,
since my light must travel far,
watch for a Nova in Pisces.
Look well, Beloved,
because across the gulf
of time and death
my newborn star will wink at you
exactly three times."

# Fragrance as Memory

My mother died when I was nine;
her face has drifted beyond memory,
past the farthest outposts of sleep,
eluding even those potent dreams
that nightly quarter a haunted land
quickening the beloved long-dead.
You are lost in eighty hollow years, Mother,
Time's Chinese boxes,
eighty orbits of the sun,
hiding your grave in his twelve houses.
But once, at fourteen,
full of grief and longing,
I crouched in a closet
scented by her clothes,
kept there by my father,
who died celibate,
faithful to white bones.
I have one handkerchief,
fragile, yellowed, lace-edged.
From it there rises,
tenuous as a shadow gliding over velvet,
a vapor-thread of her perfume,
a half-century rarefied,
to wake a grieving child.

# Leaf and Stream

A dead leaf,
Impressionist-painted,
Concave, desiccated little craft,
  Bobbing,
  Twirling,
  Rocking,
  Pirouetting,
  Capering,
  Strutting
In a kind of manic abandon
As it drifts seaward
Down a frothy leaden stream
Greylit by a pallid November sky,
One dry leaf,
Still aflame from autumn's forge:
Why does this tiny insouciant voyager
Flood my heart with tears?

# Smiles

This is an unbearable truth:
all over the world
people are smiling,
and no two smiles
are ever alike.
But the smile I loved
is no longer among them;
it will never delight me again
with its sweet radiance.
No, never on earth,
nor in the millions of smiles
immanent in the grey, empty years ahead,
gaunt lions in the path
I must now walk alone.
She whose easy, gallant smile
was like April sunshine
suddenly spilling its gold
on a bank of wildflowers,
is gone—
surely to wrest a fleeting curve
even from Charon's iron lips—
and with her went my life,
my joy,
and my own smile.

# About the Author

Arthur Porges was born in Chicago, Illinois on August 20, 1915. One of four brothers, he was educated at Roosevelt High School and Senn High School before enrolling at The Lewis Institute where he achieved a Bachelor of Science Degree in Mathematics. After the successful completion of his postgraduate studies, through which he attained Masters Degrees in Mathematics and Engineering from the Illinois Institute of Technology, Porges enlisted in the U.S. Army in 1942. During the Second World War he served as an artillery instructor, teaching algebra and trigonometry to field personnel. He was stationed at various military installations including Camp White in Oregon, Fort Sill, Oklahoma, Camp Roberts, California and at Barnes Hospital in Vancouver, Washington. After the war Porges returned to Illinois and taught mathematics at the Western Military Academy, going on to serve as an assistant professor at De Paul University. Having taught at Occidental College in Los Angeles for a brief stint in the late forties, Porges made a permanent move to California in 1951 and spent several years as a mathematics teacher at Los Angeles City College. During this period he wrote and sold short stories as a sideline. In 1957, Porges retired from teaching to write full-time. He went on to publish hundreds of short stories in numerous magazines and newspapers. Many of his stories appeared in *Alfred Hitchcock's Mystery Magazine*, *Ellery Queen's Mystery Magazine*, *Amazing Stories* and *The Magazine of Fantasy and Science Fiction*. His fiction spanned several genres, with tales ranging from science fiction and fantasy to horror, mysteries, and so on. At his most prolific his work was appearing in three or four periodicals in one month alone. Among his best known stories are "The Ruum," "The Rats," "No Killer Has Wings," "The Mirror" and "The Rescuer." Six book collections of his short stories have been published: *Three Porges Parodies and a Pastiche* (1988), *The Mirror and Other Strange Reflections* (2002), *Eight Problems in Space: The Ensign De Ruyter Stories* (2008), *The Adventures of Stately Homes and Sherman Horn* (2008), *The Calabash of Coral Island and Other Early Stories* (2008) and *The Miracle of the Bread and Other Stories* (2008). A keen birdwatcher and an avid reader, Porges also wrote many articles, essays and poems, most of which were published in *The Monterey Herald*. After spells in Laguna Beach and San Clemente, Porges moved north, eventually settling in Pacific Grove. He passed away, at the age of 90, in May 2006.

www.ingramcontent.com/pod-product-compliance
Lightning Source LLC
Chambersburg PA
CBHW031330040426
42443CB00005B/275